MW00813435

THIS SKETCHBOOK BELONGS TO ....

CONTACT ....